HAGAKURE
ILLUSTRATED
BOOK OF THE SAMURAI

HAGAKURE
ILLUSTRATED
BOOK OF THE SAMURAI

YAMAMOTO TSUNETOMO

amber
BOOKS

Copyright © 2024 Amber Books Ltd

Amber Books Ltd
United House
North Road
London N7 9DP
United Kingdom
www.amberbooks.co.uk
Facebook: amberbooks
YouTube: amberbooksltd
Instagram: amberbooksltd
X(Twitter): @amberbooks

All rights reserved. No part of this work may be reproduced, stored in a retrieval system, or transmitted in any form or by any means, electronic, mechanical, photocopying, recording, or otherwise, without the prior permission of the copyright holder.

ISBN: 978-1-83886-465-1

Translated by Melanie Clegg
Editor: Michael Spilling
Designer: Rick Fawcett
Picture Research: Terry Forshaw

Printed and bound in China

TRADITIONAL CHINESE BOOKBINDING
This book has been produced using traditional Chinese bookbinding techniques, using a method that was developed during the Ming Dynasty (1368–1644) and remained in use until the adoption of Western binding techniques in the early 1900s. In traditional Chinese binding, single sheets of paper are printed on one side only, and each sheet is folded in half, with the printed pages on the outside. The book block is then sandwiched between two boards and sewn together through punched holes close to the cut edges of the folded sheets.

Contents

Introduction	6
Bushidō & The Way	12
Etiquette & Conduct	30
Preparation & Attitude	40
Training & Self-improvement	48
Thinking, Learning & the Arts	60
Being of Service	70
Engaging with Superiors & Giving Opinions	86
Leadership & Working with Others	94
Drinking & Socializing	112
Family Relations, Youth & Aging	124
Material Possessions & Physical Presentation	140
General Advice	148
Sources and Picture Credits	160

A mounted Samurai at the battle of Sekigahara (1600). The largest battle in Japanese feudal history, Tokugawa Ieyasu gained a victory over the Toyotomi loyalists that provided the platform for establishing the long-lasting Tokugawa shogunate (1603–1869).

Introduction

In the 150-year period leading up to the 17th century, Japan was embroiled in civil war. Known as the Sengoku period, or Warring States period, this was a time when powerful regional lords across the country waged wars to expand their domains and amass power. The warrior class of samurai fought for honour and glory while the general populace suffered under the fractured system, leading to unrest and uprisings.

Three Warlords

Towards the end of the era, three major warlords emerged: Oda Nobunaga, Toyotomi Hideyoshi and Tokugawa Ieyasu. One after another, they worked to bring Japan under their rule until the country was finally unified under Tokugawa Ieyasu and entered a new age of peace and prosperity.

The shogunate government was set up in the newly appointed capital city of Edo, modern-day Tokyo, and a new political system was implemented. Some of the new rules and regulations were enacted with the aim of taming the samurai, who had previously been active warriors, and creating a new, primarily bureaucratic, role for them in a peaceful society. The two swords that samurai carried became status symbols, fulfilling a ceremonial rather than a practical role, and more emphasis was placed on prowess in literature, scholarship and the arts than on skill in combat.

A Peaceful Era

When Yamamoto Tsunetomo was born in 1659, the shogunate had already been ruling from the capital of Edo for half a century. Samurai now lived in castle towns under the close supervision of regional lords, who themselves were closely monitored by the military government through a system of 'alternate attendance' requiring their presence in Edo for half their lives.

Nabeshima Mitsushige (1632–1700) is famous for forbidding ritual suicide among his retainers, a stance that influenced Yamamoto Tsunetomo.

Urban culture flourished and pleasure districts such as the famous Yoshiwara in Edo were resplendent with geisha in painted faces, flamboyant kabuki actors and courtesans with luxurious silk kimono and elaborate hairstyles. The city bustled with merchants, booksellers, woodblock print artists, Buddhist monks and people from all over the land mingling together and creating and perfecting distinct forms of culture. The new political system was well established, and its laws governed the role of samurai in society. The practice of following one's lord into death had been banned, and many samurai now spent time cultivating the arts and enjoying their leisure time in this vibrant environment.

The Man Behind *Hagakure*

Yamamoto Tsunetomo entered into service as a samurai to lord Nabeshima Mitsushige in the Saga Domain at the age of nine. His father was Jin'uemon Shigezumi, who was already 70 years old when Tsunetomo was born and still firmly entrenched in the samurai attitudes of his age. After his father died when he was just 11, Tsunetomo's major influences came from his teacher Yamamoto Gorōzaemon and later from the monk Tannen, under whom he studied Zen Buddhism. He also studied Confucianism with a scholar called Ishida Ittei. These names crop up throughout *Hagakure* as Tsunetomo shares teachings from and anecdotes about the people who helped shape his worldview.

In his later years, following the death of his lord, Tsunetomo became a Buddhist monk. It was during this time of hermitage that he narrated his personal thoughts and philosophies to another samurai, and these were published in 1716 in a book titled *Hagakure*. The title has been translated into English as *In the Shadow of Leaves and Hidden Leaves*. It is one of five famous works of *bushidō* that emerged in the first half of the Edo Period, which also included Miyamoto Musashi's *The Book of the Five Rings*. Tsunetomo died in 1719, but his legacy has lived on in the words of *Hagakure*, providing inspiration to famous figures such as the author Yukio Mishima and motivating people in their everyday lives, not only in Japan but around the world.

The Philosophy of *Bushidō*

The philosophy of *bushidō*, or the Way of the Warrior, was developed during the Edo period as the samurai found their place in a new way of living that revolved around literacy and leisure rather than war.

Tsunetomo's personal concept of *bushidō* was deeply influenced by his father and grandfather, men from an era when samurai were a warrior class, and it's clear that he felt that the young samurai of his day had lost their way and strayed from the true warrior ethos. His core philosophy is one of accepting and even embracing death, of plunging ahead without thought for whether one lives or dies. This isn't to be mistaken for a craving for death, though; instead, the idea is that in being resolved to the idea of death, one's mind is freed from fear and therefore reaches a state of clarity which is far more likely to bring success than constant hesitation and over-planning.

Ashigaru (foot soldiers) began using musketry towards the end of the 16th century, changing the nature of warfare in Japan and undermining the supremacy of the traditional swordsman.

When it comes to action, the samurai must forge courageously ahead, though at the same time Tsunetomo encourages restraint in one's personal life and impresses the importance of correct etiquette. He also emphasizes self-denial and casting aside one's own desires in favour of complete dedication and service to one's lord. In his eyes, it is not the outcome of a task that matters, but the attitude you approach it with.

Hagakure Today

Taken at face value, the heavy focus on death and the emphasis on unquestioning commitment to one's lord that *Hagakure* recommends may not seem applicable in the modern era. However, the core philosophies are, I think, timeless. Especially in an age when many of us are plagued with anxieties from a constant bombardment of information and other distractions, the principles of single-mindedness and rigorous self-discipline can help us in focusing our mind on what truly matters. Though we may not find ourselves charging onto a battlefield with swords drawn, we can learn to dive into our own endeavours without worrying about success or failure, and to be content with knowing we have given it our all.

Beyond the spiritual and philosophical musings, some advice is also eminently practical: for example, Tsunetomo offers advice on not drinking too much at social gatherings, or how to persuade your boss that their idea is a bad one without offending them!

A Note on the Translation

The original *Hagakure* manuscript is long lost, but several handwritten copies, and copies of these copies, still exist, all with slight differences between them. Book 1 (out of 11 in total) contains around 200 anecdotes, from which I picked the ones I found to be the most relevant, interesting and accessible.

The aim of this book is not to produce a completely accurate translation of the original text, but to take its essence and transmit it in a way that will resonate with modern audiences. While the source text always serves as the foundation, liberties have been taken with the wording, and some anecdotes have been shortened or split apart. Rather than taking a chronological approach, I arranged the anecdotes by theme to make it easy to dip in and out of the book when looking for inspiration on a particular topic.

You might also notice that I have taken a gender-neutral approach. Of course, we know that samurai were generally (although not always!) male and that this was a text written for a male audience. However, the Japanese language rarely uses personal pronouns or gendered terms, making this approach true to the original wording as well as accessible to a wide audience.

I hope you find these anecdotes interesting and that they offer not only an insight into the ways of the ancient samurai, but also inspiration for your own life in the modern world.

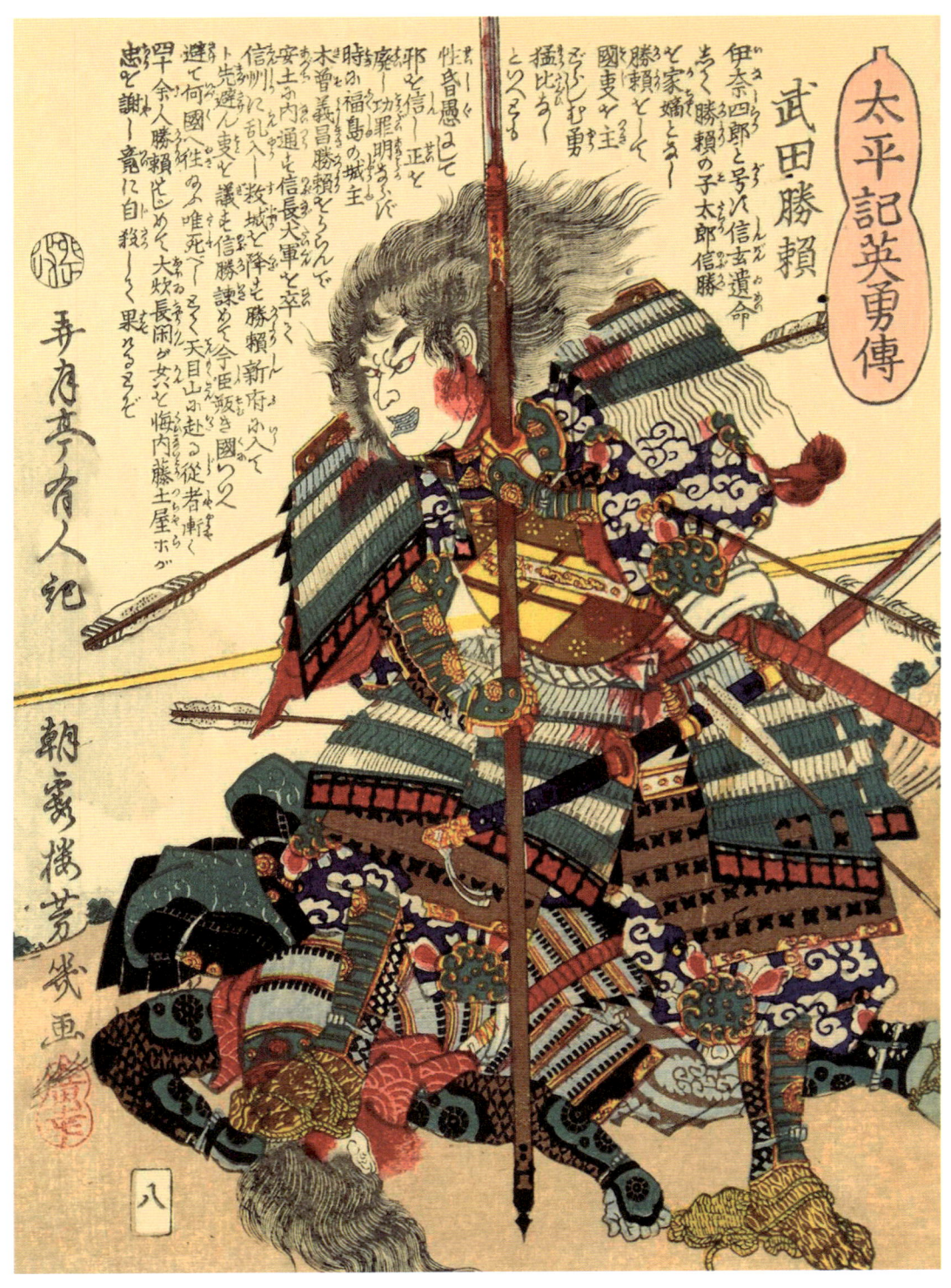

Samurai were the elite warriors of the Warring States period and beyond, skilled with the katana sword, *yari* spear (shown here) and *yumi* bow.

Bushidō & The Way

武士道

A warrior must strive to follow the Way of the Warrior, also known as *bushidō*. While this may appear obvious, it seems to me that nearly everyone is negligent in this regard. There is barely anyone who, when asked 'What do you think is the meaning of *bushidō*?', can answer right away. This is because they have not resolved themselves in their heart. And in this, we can see their neglect of *bushidō*. This is negligence in the extreme.

(Anecdote 1)

I believe that the meaning of *bushidō* is to die. By this I mean that, when forced to choose between life and death, the warrior elects to die without hesitation. No special consideration is required; the warrior simply resolves themselves and moves forward. The notionthat a person's death is in vain if they die without achieving their goals is merely a conceited veneer of *bushidō* put on by the bourgeoisie. When staring death in the face, one cannot analyse whether one will achieve one's aims. Everyone would prefer to live, and I suppose we could all come up with justifications for why we chose that course. But if you survive without that being your intention, you are a coward. You cannot count upon

Samurai engage in *Kenjutsu*, which means 'methods, techniques, and the art of the Japanese sword'.

this distinction. On the other hand, if you die without that being your intention, your death is deemed irrational, or in vain. But there is no shame in it: this is true *bushidō*. When you repeatedly face death every morning and evening, and are prepared to meet it head on, you will find freedom in *bushidō*, and you will spare yourself the shame of error and be able to fulfil your duty for as long as you live.

(*Anecdote 2*)

A retainer kneels before his *daimyo* (lord) in this photograph dating from the 1870s.

Sagara Kyuma was a man who made his own feelings in agreement with his lord's and who performed his duties with the resolve to face death. He was a mighty man who could be said to perform the work of a thousand.

(Anecdote 7)

To cultivate the Four Oaths means: not to fall behind others in the Way of the Warrior; to be resolved to display your prowess to the world; and to be of service to one's lord.

(Anecdote 19)

Looking at the retainers of today, they cast their gazes low to the ground, like sneaky pickpockets. Most of them are thinking of their own loss and gain, or else they are putting on pretences; and even those who look like they might have some nerve are always on their guard.

A person cannot call themselves a true retainer unless they are completely and utterly devoted to their lord, are resolved to die, think carefully before speaking and are focused on strengthening the domain. This applies regardless of social station.

(Anecdote 35)

'A Daimyo Talking to One of His Retainers', by artist Katsukawa Shunkō (1743–1812).

As the monk Tannen said, 'When we teach only freedom from obstructive thought, we become restless. To be free from obstructive thought means right mindfulness.' I find this very interesting. Lord Sanenori also said, 'Even a single breath should be free of evil thoughts.

That is the Way.' In other words, there is only one way.

No one has found this light from the beginning.

It is not possible to attain focused purity until

you have accumulated some achievements.

(Anecdote 39)

It is a difficult thing to maintain honour and reject dishonour.

However, placing honour above all else is in fact the cause of

a great many failures; because the Way is above honour. The

Way is a high wisdom and as such is hard to find. Looking

down from this higher plane, we can see that honour and

such concepts are mere trifles. But you can't understand

this without knowing and experiencing it for yourself.

Still, there is a means to arrive at The Way even if you can't find

it yourself, and that is by talking to others. Even if you don't

know the Way yourself, you can observe and understand what

other people are doing. It's like when people watch a game of

go and can predict the coming moves better than the players

themselves. The best way to know your own flaws is to talk to

others. Listen, learn, read books, discard your own thoughts

and follow the wisdom of those who have gone before.

(Anecdote 44)

There is nothing that cannot be achieved so long as you seek The Way. Heaven and earth can be moved by our will alone. Dedicate yourself wholeheartedly, until your tears run red with blood, and I believe it will lead you to the gods.

(Anecdote 58)

Naoshige said: '*Bushidō* is to become so frenzied by death that even a dozen warriors cannot fell you.' Great deeds can't be accomplished with an earnest mind; you have to dispense with logic and become as a madman throwing himself into the grave. When it comes to the Way of the Warrior, if you show prudence, you have already fallen behind. Don't think of loyalty or filial piety. *Bushidō* is about plunging toward certain death; loyalty and filial piety will naturally blossom within you in these circumstances.

(Anecdote 114)

'The Filial Son at Kamakura', from the series 'Twenty-Four Japanese Paragons of Filial Piety for the Honchō Circle', ca. 1821.

Yashima Gakutei (1786–1868) is best known for his *kyoka* poetry and *surimono* woodblock prints.

It is not good to be divided. Warriors must devote themselves to *bushidō*, the Way of the Warrior, and not seek anything else. This is how it is with all Ways. Still, if you try to mix *bushidō* with the teachings of Confucius and Buddha, you will not find the Way. But if you learn about other Ways while having this understanding, you will be able find the Way.

(*Anecdote 140*)

A warrior's words in the moment are very important – a single word can demonstrate courage. In a peaceful world, our courage is revealed through our words. In turbulent times, our words can show our cowardice, too. Our words are the flowers of our heart, though this concept is hard to express.

(Anecdote 142)

A warrior should make sure never to say or do anything that could be perceived as weak. The depths of a person's heart can be revealed in the slightest, most passing thing.

(Anecdote 143)

Nothing is impossible. You can move heaven and earth if you have the single-minded determination to do so. Anything is possible – it's just that most people lack the resourcefulness and resolution to do it. Effortlessly moving heaven and earth is simply a matter of willpower.

(Anecdote 144)

Shiragi Saburo, born as Minamoto no Yoshimitsu (1045–1127), was a samurai from the Minamoto clan who lived during the Heian Period. Yoshimitsu is renowned for founding the martial art *Daitō-ryū Jujutsu*.

A warrior who cares little about their reputation is inferior to one who cares a lot. People who don't care about cultivating their reputation are generally fake, deceptive, haughty and ultimately useless.

(Anecdote 155)

Kusunoki Masashige wrote: 'A warrior never surrenders, not even as a ploy or for the sake of their lord.'

(Anecdote 159)

The old warriors tell us that if we go out onto the battlefield with a desire not to be surpassed by others and strive to break through the enemy line, we will not fall behind, our hearts will be brave and we will demonstrate our valour. And if you die in battle, make sure your corpse falls forward, toward the enemy.

(Anecdote 163)

For those living the life of a warrior, dying for one's lord is a more meritorious feat than striking down the enemy. This is well illustrated in the loyal deeds of Sato Tsugunobu.

(Anecdote 172)

Two samurai advance amidst a hail of arrows. The samurai on the left wears a *sashimono*, a battle flag worn on the back of their armour as a means of identification.

'The Warrior Saga Gorō Mitsutoki', by Utagawa Kuniyoshi (1798–1861). The print shows Mitsutoki wearing protective armour from which several arrows are protruding, prostrating himself onboard a Taira ship.

According to the old warriors, a samurai should be stubborn to a fault. If you stop work on something when you think you have done 'enough', you will later gain a reputation for not doing things properly. But if you always strive to do more than enough, you will leave nothing to be desired. Always bear this in mind.

(Anecdote 189)

Once you have set your mind to accomplishing a goal, avoid the temptation to take the long way around out of fear that plunging straight ahead will lead to failure. Dragging things out will weaken your resolve, making you less likely to be successful. The Way of the Warrior necessitates speed, so act without hesitation.

(Anecdote 190)

'High-Ranking Samurai Girl with Four Attendants', from the series 'A Brocade of Eastern Manners', by Torii Kiyonaga (ca. 1784).

Etiquette & Conduct

礼儀・振舞

It is not good manners to yawn in front of people. When a yawn starts to make its presence known, stop it by rubbing your forehead. If you can't do that, wyou could try licking your lips while keeping your mouth firmly closed. Alternatively, pull your collar up over your mouth or conceal it with your sleeve so that no one notices. The same goes for sneezing; it makes you look foolish. We should watch our conduct and practise good manners in all situations.

(Anecdote 17)

Without elegance, etiquette will always fall short.

(Anecdote 32)

Someone once said of another: 'That fellow sure is strong-minded. Did you hear what he said in front of so-and-so?' This wasn't an appropriate thing to say. They only said it because they wanted to be perceived as tough, but instead they come across as shallow and immature. The beauty of a samurai is in their politeness; it is vulgar to talk like this in front of others.

(Anecdote 57)

Actors Bandō Hikosaburō as Hayano Kanpei and Sawamura Tanosuke as his wife Okaru, from the series 'The Storehouse of Loyal Retainers', by Utagawa Kuniaki II (ca. 1862).

'Samurai Fight on a Snowy mountainside', by Sadahide (1807–73).

A retainer must be alert at all hours, and always conduct themselves as if they are in the presence of their lord or in a public place. If you are seen to be careless during your down time, people might think you are careless in your work life, too. Always be aware of this.

(*Anecdote 66*)

We should never hesitate to correct our mistakes. If we address them without the slightest delay, the mistake can be erased. If, on the other hand, we attempt to cover up our mistakes, we will eventually be disgraced and we will suffer for it.

When you have said something you shouldn't have, you should quickly explain the reason why you said it. Then there will be no harm done, and there will be no need to be ashamed.

If people continue to lambast you, be prepared to tell them the following: 'I know that what I said was wrong, so I explained to you why I said it; if that is not enough for you, then there's nothing more I can do. I didn't intend to offend you, so this is the same as if you didn't even listen to me. Everyone says something they shouldn't at some point or another.'
These situations are bound to happen, so you should not speak carelessly about secrets or personal matters. Always be mindful of who is present before speaking even a single word.

(*Anecdote 90*)

A warrior should be mindful of everything and loathe to fall behind in anything. If you aren't careful in conversation, you may find yourself saying things like, 'I'm a coward', 'I would run from that situation', 'I'm scared' or 'It hurts.' These things should never pass your lips even as a joke, while half asleep or in idle chatter. People may overhear and make assumptions about you. Always have this in mind.

(*Anecdote 118*)

When a man's son was to be taken into service, the man gave his son the following advice: 'When you are at the palace, refrain from looking around the place. Resolve not to speak and remain exactly where you are seated. If someone speaks to you, answer 10 of their words with just one of your own. Do this, and you will appear resolute and steadfast. If you goggle around the place and chatter mindlessly, your inner self will be exposed, and you will come across as a careless person. This is called "sitting with the mind" and you must not forget to practise it, especially when you are becoming settled in a place.'

(*Anecdote 134*)

Man seated with his reading and writing materials before him (Edo period).

When reading a poem aloud, the flow of the verses is very important. Similarly, we must pay attention to our speech in everyday life.

(*Anecdote 141*)

My father Jin'uemon always used to say: 'A deep bow will never break your back, and your pen will never run dry from writing respectful phrases.'

People these days lack a sense of courtesy, appear careless and present themselves sloppily. It is better to show respect equally and at all times. If you are to be seated for a long time, you should bow deeply at the beginning and at the end of the meeting. While you are there, make sure to follow along with the mood and customs of the place. If you think that you are doing the proper reverence, you will fall short of it. People these days are rude and restless.

(Anecdote 145)

A mature person is one of few words. When Nabeshima Ichiun visited Nichimon, all he said was: 'Give my regards to Nabeshima Mitsushige.'

(Anecdote 185)

'The Actor Sawamura Sojuro III as a Nobleman Writing Poetry', by Katsukawa Shun'ei (ca. 1782).

A samurai on horseback with his retainers ready to launch themselves into a fight – colour woodcut by Utagawa Kunisada (1823–80).

Preparation & Attitude

覚悟・心身

Every evening, you should consider the next day and write down your plans. This is a rule to ensure you are always one step ahead of everyone else.

(Anecdote 18)

Military science makes clear the difference between being prepared and being unprepared. Being prepared is not simply about having had experience with a situation and remembering how you dealt with it. It is also about considering potential situations and making plans beforehand so that you know what to do when the time comes. In other words, a prepared person researches every option and makes decisions in advance.

For a person who is unprepared, even if a situation goes well, this can only be attributed to good luck. If you don't give appropriate consideration beforehand, then you are an unprepared person.

(Anecdote 21)

A print showing actor Sawamura Tosshō in the role of Shirai Gonpachi, a samurai turned outlaw, about to draw his sword, by Toyohara Kunichika.

There is a saying about 'the feeling of heavy rain'. If you get caught in a sudden downpour on the road, you can try to rush along the path faster or duck under the eaves to avoid getting wet, but you will still end up drenched. If you are prepared to get wet from the outset, you will get wet just the same, but it will not faze you. This mindset can be applied to all things.

(Anecdote 79)

In this confrontation on a shore, a samurai has leaped from his horse that has fallen in the mud; others fight behind him (woodcut by Utagawa Yoshitora, ca. 1870).

In most things, a 'middle of the road' approach is generally best.

However, when it comes to the martial arts, you have to go in with

the determination to be better than everyone else.

An old warrior said that if you constantly strive to surpass the feats

of experienced warriors and defeat the strongest foes, when you head into battle your heart will be brave, you will never tire and you will be able to demonstrate your valour. We should have this mindset at all times.

(*Anecdote 83*)

If you are not resolved to a decision, people can easily steamroller you. Also, if you are distracted in a meeting, you might find yourself simply going along with what other people say and agreeing with something you are not prepared for. You might absentmindedly nod and say yes, and people will think you are on board. So, when in meetings and discussions, make sure never to let your guard down for even a second.

Make sure not to let yourself be manipulated when someone is telling or giving you something. Don't go along with something you're not happy with; be ready to speak up about your misgivings and point out the issues. Be careful, because differences of opinion can arise around not just big issues, but small ones, too.

Also, it's better to stay away from people you are not sure about, because they can trip you up and drag you into things. You will need to experience this before you can properly understand it.

(Anecdote 86)

Death is easy enough to face if we are always prepared for it. It is a waste of time to worry about the future; calamities, when they happen, are never as bad as you imagined. Make peace with the fact that the ultimate fate of a samurai is either to become a *rōnin* or to perform *seppuku*.

(*Anecdote 92*)

It is not enough to face hardships with a calm demeanour. Instead, we should meet these difficulties with joy and open arms. This will take you a step up. As the saying goes: when the water rises, so does the ship.

(*Anecdote 116*)

The best way to surpass others is to talk to them about your own ideas and ask for their advice. Most people rely only on their own logic, and so they cannot surpass others. Simply consulting someone else will raise you a step up. I remember how a person consulted me about writing an official document. Though they were a more skilled researcher and writer than me, they demonstrated their superiority over others by asking me to look it over.

(*Anecdote 138*)

Actor Matsumoto Kōshirō V plays a samurai at an open-air tea house, holding a pipe with his smoking kit at his side (colour woodcut by Utagawa Toyokuni, ca. 1815).

Training & Self-improvement

修業

An expert swordsman once said: 'Throughout life there is an order to acquiring knowledge. You start out at the bottom, where no matter how much you train, you still struggle, and you think yourself inadequate – at this point, other people will think you are, too. You're of no use to anyone at this stage. When you reach the mid-level, you're still useless, but you are aware of your own need to improve, and this is obvious to other people. As you rise up the ranks, you will grow into your own, gain confidence, be pleased to hear praise from others and feel disappointed when other people can't measure up to you. Now, you are useful. Then, when you become the cream of the crop, you will act like you don't know things, but people will still be amazed by your skill. This is where most people plateau. But above this, there is a level for which there is no premade path. Make your way far enough down it, and you will understand that there is no end to learning, and that you can never be fully satisfied. Once you fully embrace your shortcomings, you will continue along the path of life without pride or self-deprecation, always striving for more. As Lord Yagyū said: "I don't know how to beat other people, but I know how to beat myself." You must go through life making sure that you are better today than you were yesterday, then better than you were today. The pursuit of knowledge is an endless endeavour.'

(*Anecdote 45*)

The boy in this tapestry hanging scroll is an immortal servant. The bald old man with a prominent forehead is the God of Longevity, and the plate of peaches in the boy's hands a symbol of immortality.

'Three Gods of Good Fortune Visit the Yoshiwara',
by Chōbunsai Eishi, early 19th century.

How should you respond when asked 'What is the most important thing to focus on in one's training?' I would say that the answer is to face the present moment in earnest. Most people seem to go through life looking defeated. It is when you strive in earnest that you will look truly alive. As you take on tasks with this attitude, something will

blossom inside you: loyalty to your lord, filial piety to your

parents, valour in martial arts and more. It will become

a means of coping with anything life throws at you.

Finding this special thing is difficult and, even if

you do find it, it's also difficult to hold onto. All we

can do is be present in the current moment.

(*Anecdote 61*)

Ishida Ittei said: 'Poor handwriting can be improved by diligently attempting to copy a beautiful hand.' In the same way, a retainer can also improve by following the example of a good retainer. These days, there is no prime exemplar of a retainer, so you will have to construct your own to learn from. To do this, select the best traits of each person from a number of people and combine them: the perfect etiquette of this person, the courage of that one, the way of speaking of another, the way this person carries themselves, this one's conscientiousness and that one's quick decision-making. When it comes to the arts, many disciples fail to reach the potential of their masters; they simply mimic them and, in doing so, also inherit their flaws, which means they never blossom in their own right. When imitating someone who is polite but neglectful of their duties, if you are not careful, you risk merely imitating the neglectfulness and disregarding the politeness. Focus only on a person's good characteristics, and anyone can be a good role model.'

(Anecdote 64)

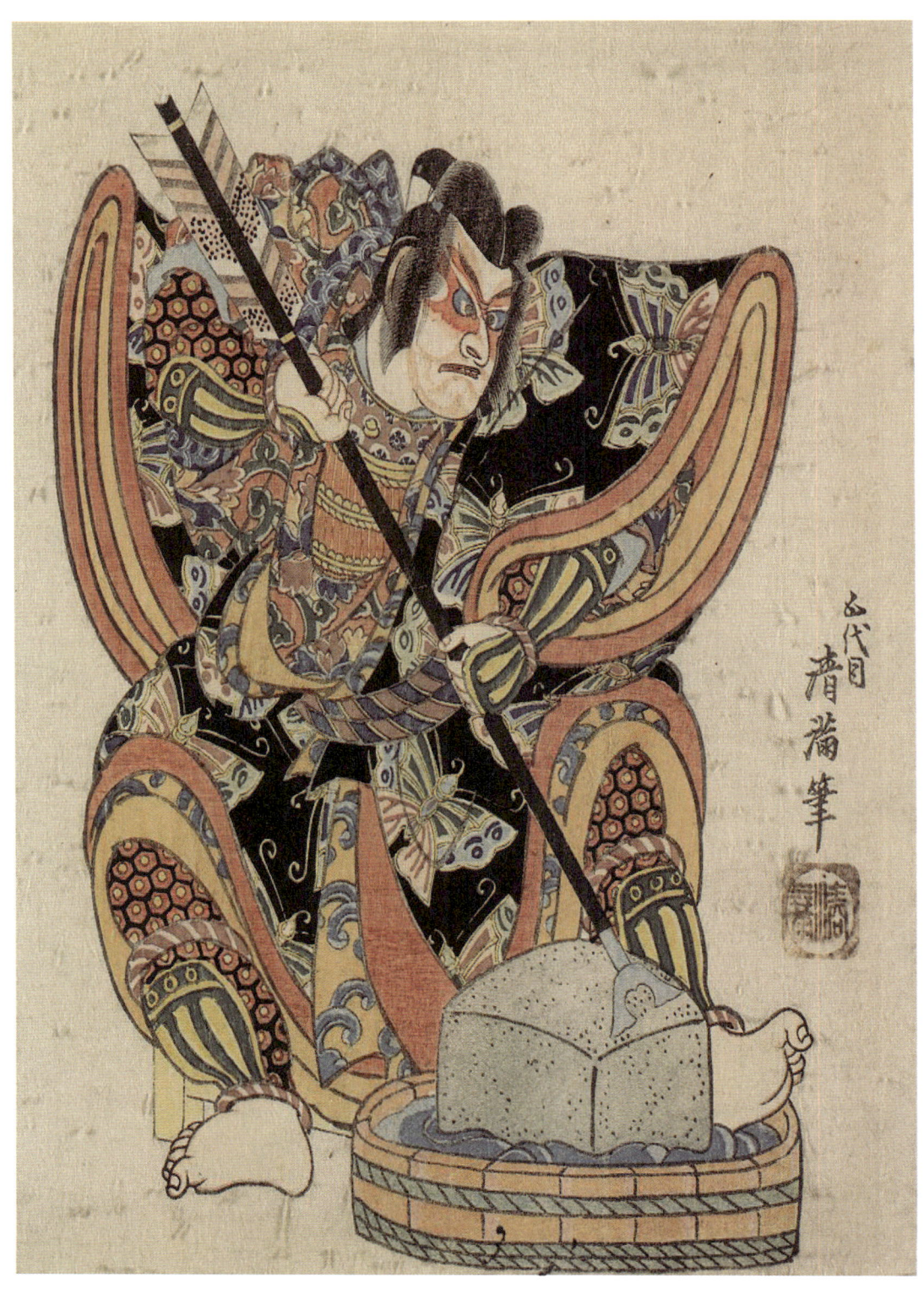

An actor portraying Yanone Goro sharpening a spear, 1823.

Many people think that simply immersing themselves in the martial arts and taking on apprentices makes them a 'warrior'. It seems a waste to push oneself so hard only to become an 'artist'. The arts are something that anyone can become proficient in if they apply themselves to learning them. Often, those who are proficient in many things come across as unrefined, and their knowledge on the crucial matters ends up half-baked.

(*Anecdote 70*)

It is cowardly to look at the deeds of an expert and think that you are no match for them. Even an expert is human, just like you are. Once you set out with the attitude of 'why should they beat me at this?', you will be headed down the right path.

(*Anecdote 117*)

Above & opposite: 'A Show of Horsemanship' (17th century screen). During the Edo period, 18 military techniques were considered essential for the proper training of a samurai. Foremost among these were horsemanship. Affluent warriors commissioned lavish folding screens that illustrated their favourite martial pastime.

The last line of a poem poses the following useful query: 'How will you answer when your own heart asks the question?' All the modern intelligentsia with their clever talk do is put on airs and muddy the waters. This is why they are inferior to those who would appear less clever: stupid people are at least forthright. If we do as the poem suggests and look into our own hearts, there will be nowhere to hide. It plays the role of judge well, and we must aim not to act shamefully before this inner judge.

(*Anecdote 40*)

Ushiwakamaru (Yoshitsune as a young boy) is fencing with Tengu, a long-nosed goblin, using wooden swords near Mount Kurimu.

You will never achieve fulfilment in your practice; to think you have finished training is to run counter to the Way. You should continuously feel that you are not yet there, right up until you draw your last breath. Only with hindsight will you be seen as accomplished in the Way.

It is very difficult to devote yourself purely and wholeheartedly to a single pursuit for your entire life; but if it is diluted by other concerns, it is not the Way. A retainer should strive to intensively devote themselves to the martial arts.

(Anecdote 139)

When I was young, I had a diary that I named my 'Journal of Regrets'. Each day I would write down the mistakes I'd made that day; every day there were at least 20 or 30 of them. It seemed there was no end to my errors, so eventually I stopped. Even now, when I reflect on the day while lying in bed at night, there's not a day that goes by without my having erred in speech or action. I just can't seem to get things right. This is something that people who manage to go through life relying on their talents won't understand.

(Anecdote 173)

This late 18th century illustration by Katsukawa Shun'ei depicts the young *daimyo* Momonoi Wakasanosuke about to draw his *katana*.

Thinking, Learning & the Arts

思考・知恵・芸能

Some people are born with an intrinsic wisdom enabling them to react in the moment, while others will come up with a solution only later when lying awake at night thinking over the situation. Although we are all born with differing abilities, if you stand upon the Four Oaths as your bedrock and think selflessly, you'll find that the answers mysteriously come to you. People often believe that if they think deeply enough on a matter, they'll eventually hit upon something profound. However, thinking based only on one's own selfishness will ultimately lead you down a path of distorted and evil thought, and nothing good can come from it. Humans are foolish creatures; it is hard for us to relinquish the self. Still, when faced with a problem, the first thing to consider is not the issue itself but the Four Oaths. Put the self aside, and you will not go far wrong.

(Anecdote 4)

When we encounter the world through the lens of our own assumptions and knowledge, our self-centredness reveals itself, we turn from the right path and we fall into evil. From an outside perspective, this is an unreliable and narrow-minded approach that is not at all helpful. When you can't come up with a straight and true answer on your own, it's best to talk to someone else who has the wisdom you seek. As an unrelated third party, they will be able to consider things selflessly

A depiction of a rōnin, or rogue samurai, by Ippitsusai Bunchō (1725–94).

and make decisions with unbiased wisdom. Then, you will find yourself on the correct path. This method is steadfast and reliable, like a great tree with many sturdy roots, while a single person's wisdom is like a sapling stuck into the ground without a root to be seen.

(*Anecdote 5*)

Jurōjin, by Kano Tanshin Moromichi, early 19th century. Jurōjin is shown as an old man with a long beard. He carries a staff and is accompanied by a deer. In Japan he is numbered as one of seven lucky gods.

Learning from the maxims and work of people from the past lets us rely upon their wisdom and prevents us from becoming self-centred. Discard your own emotions and preconceptions, listen to the maxims of the past, converse with other people… and you will do well.

(Anecdote 6)

Lord Naoshige wrote in his book *O-Kabegaki*: 'Think lightly on weighty matters.' Ishida Ittei added an annotation: 'And think deeply on minor matters.'

(Anecdote 46)

As the priest Kōnan Oshō warned, education and studying are good things, but they can also lead to mistakes. Studying is useful when you take what you have read and apply it to discovering your own deficiencies. However, this is difficult to do. Often, studying leads people to have a high opinion of themselves and to act as though they know everything.

(Anecdote 72)

'Any artistic pursuit can be beneficial if it is done for the sake of your work. However, many people will end up obsessed with the art for art's sake. Any form of study can be dangerous in this regard.

(Anecdote 80)

There is an ancient saying: 'Think and decide in seven breaths.' Lord Takanobu said: 'Even wise judgement loses its clarity when it takes its time.' Lord Naoshige said: 'Nine times out of 10, it is not good to take your time. A warrior does things quickly.' When you give your mind time to wander, it will not land on a decision. Be clear and motivated, do not dawdle and you will come to a decision within seven breaths. This is a state of mind that embodies courage and swift breakthroughs.

(Anecdote 122)

People who have a modicum of intelligence tend to make light of the present circumstances. This is a source of misfortune. People who are careful with their words are useful in good times and will avoid legal troubles when times are turbulent.

(Anecdote 135)

'Onoe Matsusuke I Talking to Nakamura Nakazo I as a Samurai',
by Torii Kiyonaga Japanese (ca. 1788).

A person who is skilled in the arts comes across as foolish, as you can only become proficient in an art by fixating on it to the detriment of everything else. In this sense, they are no good at anything.

(Anecdote 147)

Shibaraku, a popular hero, as depicted by Torii Kiyomasu (ca. 1716).

There are no worthy people these days. People don't even listen to advice that will help them succeed, let alone put it into practice. I've met people all over the place, and they all moderate their speech, perhaps afraid of ridicule if they speak their mind fully.

(Anecdote 167)

The monk Tannen said: 'A retainer who is too clever will not succeed; still, neither will a stupid one.'

(Anecdote 180)

When faced with an important matter, even if you do not fully understand it, first you must think. Then, using your ideas as your foundation, forge ahead without hesitation and see it through to the bitter end; otherwise, you will get nowhere. When consulting other people, you will often find that they turn their back on you, or don't tell it to you straight. That's why your own judgement is never more important than in these times. At any rate, if you simply decide to cast your self aside and plunge into things with wild abandon, it will be a piece of cake. If you try to meticulously plan how best to do things, you'll start to second-guess yourself and probably fail.

(Anecdote 194)

'Minamoto Yoshitsune and His Retainer, the Monk Benkei, Putting to Flight the Ghost of Taira no Tomomori', by Kuwagata Keisai (late 18th century).

Being of Service

奉
職

The ideal retainer is one who single-mindedly serves and cherishes their lord. If you also happen to find yourself possessing wit, talent or other such gifts, then you are truly blessed. Even if you do not excel at anything, so long as you have the inner resolve to cherish and serve, you will be a retainer whose lord relies upon them. A retainer who relies only on their wit and talent is not a good one.

(Anecdote 3)

A retainer who is their lord's ally, who leaves the judgement of right and wrong up to them, and who discards their own self in order to serve cannot possibly offer any more than this. If a lord has but two or three retainers of this calibre, their house will be in order.

(Anecdote 9)

When you are asked to do something, whether it be something you want to do or not, you will appear confused if you say nothing. You should give some kind of response, so it is best to be prepared and think about what you will say in advance. If you feel secretly pleased and proud when asked to fulfil a role, it will show on your face. I've seen this happen to people, and it is never a good look. For those who are aware of their own shortcomings, and who believe themselves to be unsuited to the task and are stressed about how to

'The Actor Segawa Kichiji plays a Daimyo's Young Son, with Sanogawa Ichimatsu as a Samurai Attendant', by Ishikawa Toyonobu (ca. 1750).

go about completing it, this too will be obvious on their face without them having to say it aloud, and they will come across as more mature. People who go into a task with excitable confidence and immediately get carried away will appear not to know what they are doing, will make mistakes and, ultimately, will probably fail at it.

(*Anecdote 71*)

It is cowardly to be afraid of not being able to fulfil a role that has been assigned to you. As the person in that role, you are bound to mess up at some point. That being said, it is shameful to mess up in your personal life. Be humble and ask yourself what you can do to serve despite your shortcomings.

(Anecdote 93)

Someone who is decently smart will gradually become conceited. Praise that they are a cut above the rest will go to their head, and they will start to openly express the opinion that they are naturally better than other people. They will come to believe that no one can surpass them, and then they will find that karma punishes them.

Even if it's true that there is something you are better at than the average person, if you have a sense of self-importance people will not like you, and you will not be useful. A person who likes to be of service to others is humble and respectful, and someone who enjoys being with others regardless of their rank will be liked by all.

(Anecdote 123)

Do not panic if you are dismissed from service. People in Lord Katsushige's time said: 'You are not a true retainer until you have been made a *rōnin* seven times. Fall down seven times and get up eight.' Naridomi Hyogo was a *rōnin* seven times. Think of it as being like a self-righting doll. Your lord may even dismiss you as a test.

(*Anecdote 128*)

So long as you carefully consider the essential aspects of the role you are given to fulfil, perform it with great care and dedication as though you are always in the presence of your lord, and live every day as though it is your last, you will not go wrong. It is said that a person fulfils their true purpose by performing their duty. For that reason, we all must find a role.

(*Anecdote 157*)

A retainer should love to serve. It is cowardly to try to shirk a big role out of fear. To take on a role and fail at it even though you tried your best is as noble as meeting your death in battle.

(*Anecdote 160*)

Even if they get things right nine times out of 10, people who are selective in the duties they take on, try to guess at their superiors' moods or work only for their own benefit will embarrassingly meet their downfall after messing up just once. This is because they are motivated by self-serving desires and lack a firm sense of loyalty.

(Anecdote 161)

To be generous means to have great compassion. A sacred verse says: 'To the compassionate eye, no one is to be despised; and so have mercy on the sinner.' Compassion is limitless and boundless. It is universal. The sages of the ancient kingdoms are still revered today because of the vastness of their compassion. Live your life for the sake of your parents, the people around you and the generations yet to come. That is great compassion. Courage and wisdom born from compassion is the real deal. Do your work out of compassion and deal punishment out of compassion, and you will be infinitely virtuous. To do things merely for your own benefit is petty and narrow-minded and nothing good will come of it. Though I learned the value of courage and wisdom a long time ago, it's only recently that I have come to understand compassion. Tokugawa Ieyasu said: 'When I think of my retainers as my children, they look to me as a father; as such, the foundation of peace is compassion.'

(Anecdote 179)

Expecting orders from his warlord Nitta Yoshioki, the samurai Yura Hyogo is shown seated inside his military camp near Hodogaya in 1358. The messenger before him brings bad news that Yoshioki is dead, betrayed by a former retainer.

'Boys Play-acting a *Daimyo* Procession', by Utagawa Kuniyoshi (19th century). In the Edo period (1603–1867), the Tokugawa shogunate established a policy by which the *daimyo* of each domain had to reside in Edo in alternate years. When the lords journeyed between Edo and their respective provinces, *daimyo* processions were an opportunity for the ruler of each domain to show off their prestige and wealth.

Yamasaki Kurando famously said: 'A retainer who is too perceptive is not a good one.' I don't like to focus on ideas of what's right and wrong, proper and improper, honourable and dishonourable, loyal and disloyal. If you love to serve, even if what is asked of you is unreasonable or your actions are ineffective, and you value your lord above all else, that is all that's required from you. That's what makes a good retainer. Perhaps you make mistakes because you are over-eager or out of excessive concern for your lord, but you will be fulfilling your long-cherished ambition. People say that too much of anything is a bad thing, but when it comes to service, there is nothing wrong with mistakes made out of overzealousness.

It's sad how people who rely only on logic tend to get hung up on small things and end up wasting their entire lives. Life is short; it is best to simply rush headlong into it. Don't let yourself be held back by distractions; immerse yourself in service and abandon all other concerns. There is no time for splitting hairs over concepts of loyalty and honour.

(Anecdote 196)

This portrait photograph taken in the 1860s shows a samurai and his retainer travelling in the snow.

'Young Woman at Night accompanied by a Servant Carrying a Lantern and a Shamisen Box', by Kitagawa Kikumaro.

Furukawa Rokurōzaemon said: 'There isn't a lord alive who doesn't wish for loyal subordinates. Even humble warriors like myself want good followers, so I'm sure that the more important you are, the more strongly you want them. So, if you want to be of service to such a person, you will certainly be useful to them as your wants are in alignment. If someone offers you something that you want, jump at the chance and take it. In my old age

I've finally realized that people can waste their whole lives by not being aware of this. Young people should always be on the alert.' This advice resonated with me, and I remember it well. Don't waste time waffling – you simply need a desire to serve. It's not that most people don't want this, but that there are many obstacles blocking the way, and we can waste our whole lives if we can't break through them. It's a real shame when this happens. Some people live in a state of constant self-deprecation, wondering how a person like them can possibly be of use. But it's okay if you aren't good at your role so long as you truly and earnestly wish to serve. Sometimes wisdom and intelligence can actually be a detriment. A lowly person out in the sticks will often view clan elders and important statespeople as mysterious and incomprehensible and so keep their distance out of respect. But if they get to know these people, they will see that there is no real difference between them, except for their unwavering devotion to their duties. You don't need any esoteric knowledge to be useful. Even fools like us can aspire to do what is best for the lord, the clan and the people. Having said that, finding that inner drive to serve is the real challenge.

(Anecdote 200)

Samurai and servant, courtesans and merchants in the pleasure quarters of Edo. Woodblock print by Masanobu Okumura (1686–1764).

Yukimori (1543–76), a samurai known for his great strength and loyalty, served the Amako *daimyo* during the Sengoku period, a time of constant civil war and social upheaval.

Engaging with Superiors & Giving Opinions

上司との交流

Samurai Isogai Tōsuke is depicted here in the vendetta play 'Revenge in Front of the Palace' (*Mido mae no adauchi*).

It is the greatest act of loyalty to correct your lord's way of thinking often and to ensure that they are free from error. First and foremost, it's best to ensure that the lord is educated in matters of their clan and ancestors from a young age. Passing on these teachings is very important.

(*Anecdote 52*)

There are many ways to present criticism to your lord. An admonition that comes from the heart should be done discreetly. When helping your lord to fix a fault, be careful not to anger or offend them.

(Anecdote 111)

If you are not in a position to admonish someone, you can demonstrate your loyalty by speaking to those who are in such a position so that the mistake can be corrected. To gain people's ear, you must get along well with others; but if you do it only for your own gain, it is just a form of sucking up. It should instead come from a sense of duty.

(Anecdote 124)

'If I give my opinion, they will only dig their heels in further, and I'll end up doing more harm than good. Therefore, I won't speak up, and I will go along with whatever I am told even if I disagree.' This way of thinking is nothing more than an excuse. If you speak with conviction, people will listen. Speak half-heartedly and people will interrupt you and oppose you, and you will end up backing down.

(Anecdote 137)

Samurai ethics were portrayed in the Kabuki theatre and in prints drawn from Kabuki such as this one, depicting the actor Ichikawa Kuzo in the role of Sanzo. He is dancing in honour of the god Daikoku, deity of fortune and wealth, in the play 'Maimosu Iro no Tanemaki' (1841).

You should be on friendly terms with the people who work closely with your superiors; but don't do this for your own benefit, because that is just sucking up. These people can serve as a ladder for when you have something you want to say to someone above you. However, it does not work unless that person is truly loyal. Everything should be done for the sake of the lord.

(Anecdote 151)

The most important thing when offering criticism is your delivery. If you go in with an attitude of trying to put everything in order down to the last tiny detail, you won't be heeded and may end up doing more harm than good. Tell them, 'You're free to do whatever you like when it comes to your leisure. If you wish for the peace and prosperity of those working for you, they will naturally be eager to serve, and your house and domain will be in order. This should not place any burden on you.' They will surely understand. Admonitions and opinions are only useful if they come after careful discussion and are based on the Way of Harmony. If you take a judgemental tone and a rigid view of the correct approach, it will result in an argument and you won't be able to fix even the simplest of things.

(Anecdote 153)

A person recorded the following in their notes:

Those who work closely with the lord should be discreet in their conduct, for a lord will be judged by those who serve beside them.

Any admonitions must be delivered in a timely manner. If you decide to wait for another opportunity because the lord is in a bad mood right now, they can make a grave mistake during that time. It is also dishonourable to speak ill of those who have been accused of misdeeds. Likewise, it's fine not to say anything about those for whom things are going well. It is a samurai's duty to take pity on those who have fallen on hard times and help them get back on their feet.

(Anecdote 192)

A samurai bides his time from behind a rock, watching as another samurai charges past (by Ogata Gekko, 1859–1920).

Leadership & Working with Others

職場の関係

It is not only important but also compassionate to present your opinions to people in order to help them fix their flaws, and it is also your duty as a retainer. Still, you must think deeply on how to deliver this critique. It's easy enough to speak on the right or wrong of a person's actions – and easy, too, to give opinions on this. People might think they are doing a kindness by bringing up a topic that others would hesitate to broach, but if this advice is not taken on board by the recipient, the advice-giver might become resigned to the belief that there's nothing they can do about it – and then they're of no help at all. It's the same as purposefully embarrassing someone or speaking ill of them; you're just saying it to make yourself feel better.

In offering a critical opinion, you must first determine whether the other person will be willing to listen to it. Make sure you are close enough to them and have built up trust over a period of time so that they are more likely to listen to you. Appeal to their personal tastes and adjust your manner of delivery. Consider the right time to bring it up, and the manner; for example, you could write a letter, or mention it as you are taking your leave. Other tactics are to bring up your own shortcomings and lead the other person to what you want to say without having to say it directly. Or get them in a good mood through flattery then skilfully implement your scheme, persuading

This box cover depicts a nighttime scene at a bustling shop, with an array of people, including samurai, a woman and her attendant, and a monk holding a fan.

them with a manner like a drink of cool water to a parched throat.

This is the kind of critique that can successfully fix someone's faults.

This is very difficult to pull off. If the flaw you are trying to fix is a habit ingrained over a long time, it won't be completely cured with one conversation. I have experienced this myself. To be a truly compassionate retainer, you should get along with your colleagues every day, correct each other's bad habits and unite to serve your lord. After all, we cannot expect someone to fix their flaws simply by shaming them.

(*Anecdote 14*)

When a young person does well in their work, even if it is only

a trifling matter, we should notice and praise them in order

to lift their spirits and induce them to progress further.

(*Anecdote 16*)

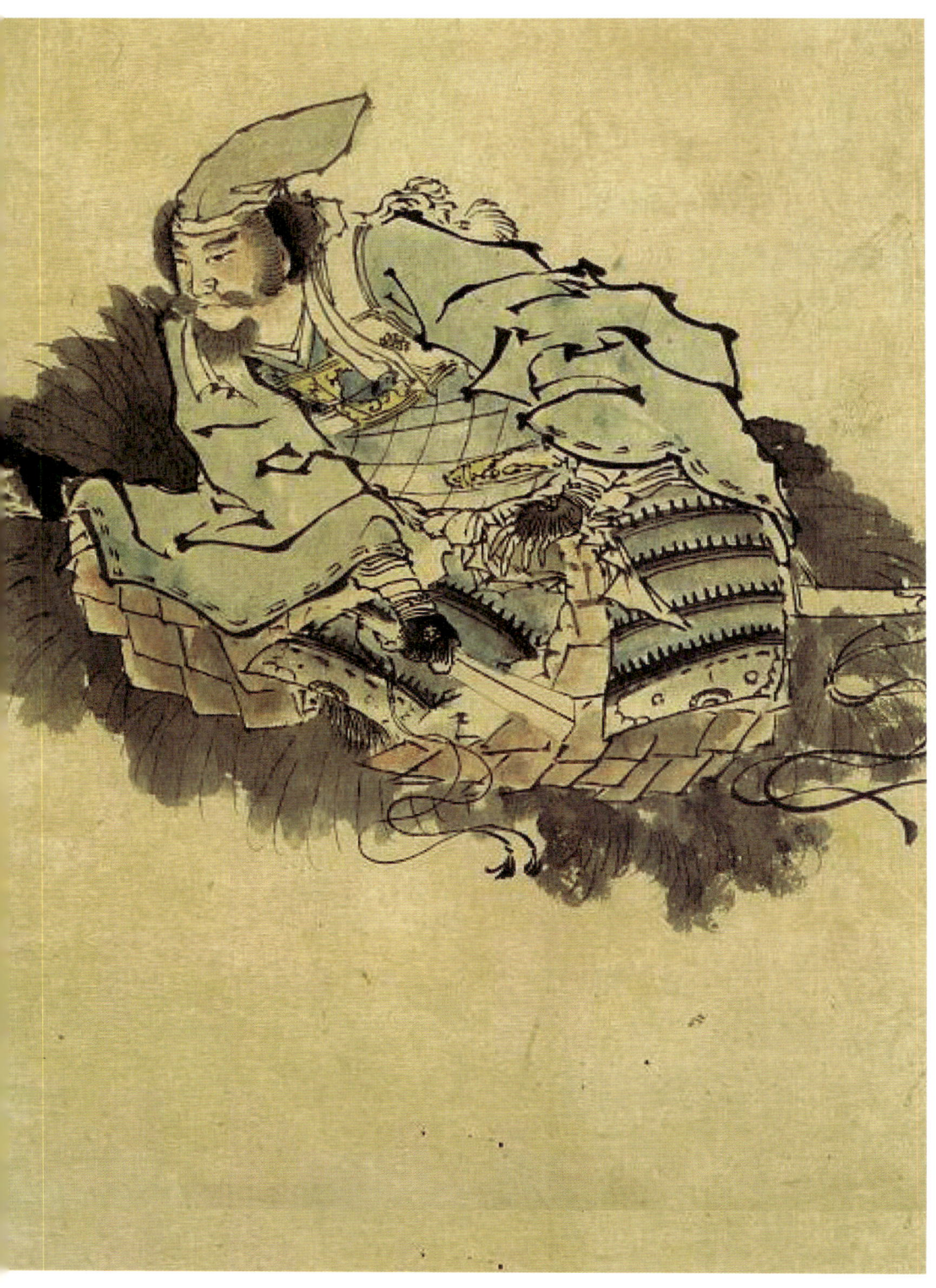

An elder samurai observes a young warrior who is armed with bow and arrows.

In many situations, it comes across as disloyal if you try to admonish someone when it is not your station to do so. To get things done, a genuinely sincere person will instead privately discuss it with the appropriate person and have that person then present it as their idea. This is true loyalty. If the first person you talk with doesn't agree, seek out someone else and carefully do what you can to ensure the crucial thing happens; but make sure to keep this great loyalty quiet from others. If you talk with many people and none of them will help, you can drop the issue; or, if you keep pushing and pushing, you will probably get

Above & opposite: Detail of a meeting between a samurai and a nobleman, from 'The Tale of Heiji Emaki' (*Heiji Monogatari Emaki*), an illuminated 13th century manuscript that narrates events of the Heiji rebellion (1159–60).

there in the end. You will never achieve your aims if you are thinking only of receiving praise for yourself and claiming the merit for your own. There are many people who talk freely but achieve nothing except for their own destruction and the ire of others, all because their intentions are insincere. But cast aside the self and think only of how to improve things for your lord, and it is plain sailing.

(*Anecdote 43*)

When discussing a potential promotion, it was unanimously decided that the man should not be promoted because he had previously behaved badly while drunk. But one person disagreed, saying: 'If we reject anyone who has ever made a single mistake, there will be no one left. A person who has made a mistake will regret it, reflect on it and learn from it to become a better subordinate. We should promote him.' Another person asked if the first was willing to guarantee the man, and they answered that they would. Everyone wanted to know why they would be so willing to put themselves on the line for this man, to which they responded: 'Precisely because he has made a mistake. Someone who has never erred is a far riskier prospect.' And so, the man was promoted.

(Anecdote 50)

People who step beyond the bounds of their station, regardless of their rank, will eventually do something cowardly or despicable; if they are of a lower rank, they will no doubt flee from their mistake. Keep an eye on those who rank below you.

(Anecdote 69)

Sometimes, a person visiting a governmental office or some such place where the staff are very busy will talk at length about their own affairs without any thought to other people. Some staff will

In this scene from a play, Bannai, retainer of Moronao, offers presents to appease his lord, watched by Honzo at left (ca. 1835–39).

get annoyed at the inconvenience, but this is not acceptable. It is the manner of a samurai to remain calm and to deal with people professionally in such a situation. To exacerbate the situation and get into an argument is a frivolous waste of time.

(*Anecdote 77*)

If one of his servants did something wrong, Yamamoto Jin'uemon would keep them on as normal for the rest of the year then, at the end of the year, dismiss them without incident.

(*Anecdote 96*)

A leader should closely study the human face. It is said that Kusunoki Masashige gave Masatsura a scroll filled with nothing but pictures of eyes. There is a secret art to interpreting a person's countenance.

(Anecdote 104)

Educating others to produce good retainers is an act of loyalty. Teach those with ambition. Great satisfaction can come from having one's own work put to use through others.

(Anecdote 125)

Just as Lord Naoshige thought, a samurai with an ambition to serve will make sure to get along well with their colleagues. I have always been friendly with everyone, from the samurai to the low-ranking foot soldiers. I figured that when the need arose, these people would step up for me. All I would have to do was ask if they would go along with me for our lord's sake, and they would do it without argument. This in turn benefits the lord by ensuring that he has good and loyal retainers.

(Anecdote 130)

'Oishi Kuranosuke Yoshio, Leader of the Forty-Seven Loyal Retainers', 1881.

In Lord Yoshitsune's book of military poems there is the following line: 'A general should communicate well with others.' This applies in times of crisis, but also in everyday life. Then, when the leader tells their followers 'You have done well so far. You have proved your worth, and now I ask just a little more of you,' they will lay down their lives.

Words carry a great weight.

(*Anecdote 131*)

Samurai direct foot soldiers as they build up shore defences (colour woodcut by Yoshitora, 1847–50).

The actor Bandō Mitsugorō in the role of Satsumanokami Tadanori, by Utagawa Kuniyasu, 1794–1832.

Yamamoto Jin'uemon always said that the most important thing for a samurai is to have followers. No matter how hard you push yourself, a person cannot win a war alone. If you need money, you can easily borrow it, but a loyal following can't be so easily gathered at short notice. You must take good care of your people on a daily basis. As a leader, you can't feed only yourself; share your rice with those in your service, and they will follow you.

(Anecdote 132)

A wise ruler heeds criticism from others. Then, when the time comes, their people will rise to the occasion and say and do whatever needs to be done, and their domain will be in order. A warrior who depends on their friends and colleagues, gets along with them, asks the knowledgeable for their opinions, recognizes their own shortcomings and constantly seeks the Way throughout life will be a treasure to their kingdom.

(Anecdote 148)

'Takeda Kōunsai at Mt. Tsukuba' by Utagawa Kuniteru III. Rebel samurai under the *Sonno Joi* ('Revere the emperor, expel the barbarians') banner gather during the Mito Rebellion (1864).

We should be grateful when people express their opinions even if they are ultimately unhelpful. Listen and absorb what they have to say and thank them for it. If you don't, they will stop sharing things they have seen or heard. It is best to create an atmosphere where people are free to speak their minds, regardless of your feelings on the matter.

(Anecdote 152)

Try to view everything from a higher position than other people. If we all drag our feet in the same place, all we'll do is butt heads and grumble and complain, and no one will see the situation clearly.

(Anecdote 165)

A leader should show kindness to the members of their group. When Nakano Kazuma served in an important post, he was so busy throughout his tenure that he never had time to visit his men. But when one of them was sick or in trouble, he made sure to drop in on them on his way home from the castle. This is why they all looked up to him.

(Anecdote 187)

Three men having a picnic under flowering plum trees (scroll painting, Indian ink and natural paint on silk).

Drinking & Socializing

飲酒・付き合い

The night before you are due to meet up with someone, you should think about where you are going, who you are meeting, how you will greet them, the sequence of events – anything and everything.

This is good manners.

When you are called to meet with a superior, if you go with the mindset that it is an inconvenience, you'll find that you spend the whole time wishing you were somewhere else. Instead, attend with the mindset that you're grateful for the invite, and you will have a good time.

In most cases, it's best not to turn up somewhere uninvited if you have no business there. When you are invited, you should behave as a good guest, lest you become an unwelcome one. Whatever the case, it's important to think beforehand about how to conduct yourself – especially if it will involve alcohol. The timing of when you leave is crucial; don't overstay, but at the same time, don't leave too early.

In general, it's best not to refuse too many offers of food or drink. Say no thank you once or twice but accept any further offers. The same goes for when you are unexpectedly required to stay somewhere.

(*Anecdote 18*)

'On a Balcony a Woman is Seated Playing a Tsuzumi, below a Man in *Daimyo* Costume is Seated upon a Black Lacquer Box' (woodblock print by Torii Kiyonaga).

When a man was to accompany his lord to his domain, he said the following: 'As I know that when we get to the countryside there will probably be a lot of drinking, I have decided that I will be very careful about it. If I say I'm not drinking, people will assume I have some kind of alcohol problem, so instead I'll say that it just doesn't agree with me. They can keep offering me drinks, but I'll keep tossing them away until they eventually stop pressuring me. I'll also be on my best, most polite behaviour and I will not speak unless spoken to.' I think that this man has the right idea. Making plans ahead of time is the first step to getting ahead of other people.

(Anecdote 38)

There are a lot of people who mess up by drinking too much. It's really unfortunate. You should get a good handle on how much you can drink and try not to drink any more than that. Still, there will be times when you overdo it. When out drinking, stay alert and think in advance of how you will react in the event of an unexpected occurrence. Also, bear in mind that you are in public, and act as such.

(Anecdote 68)

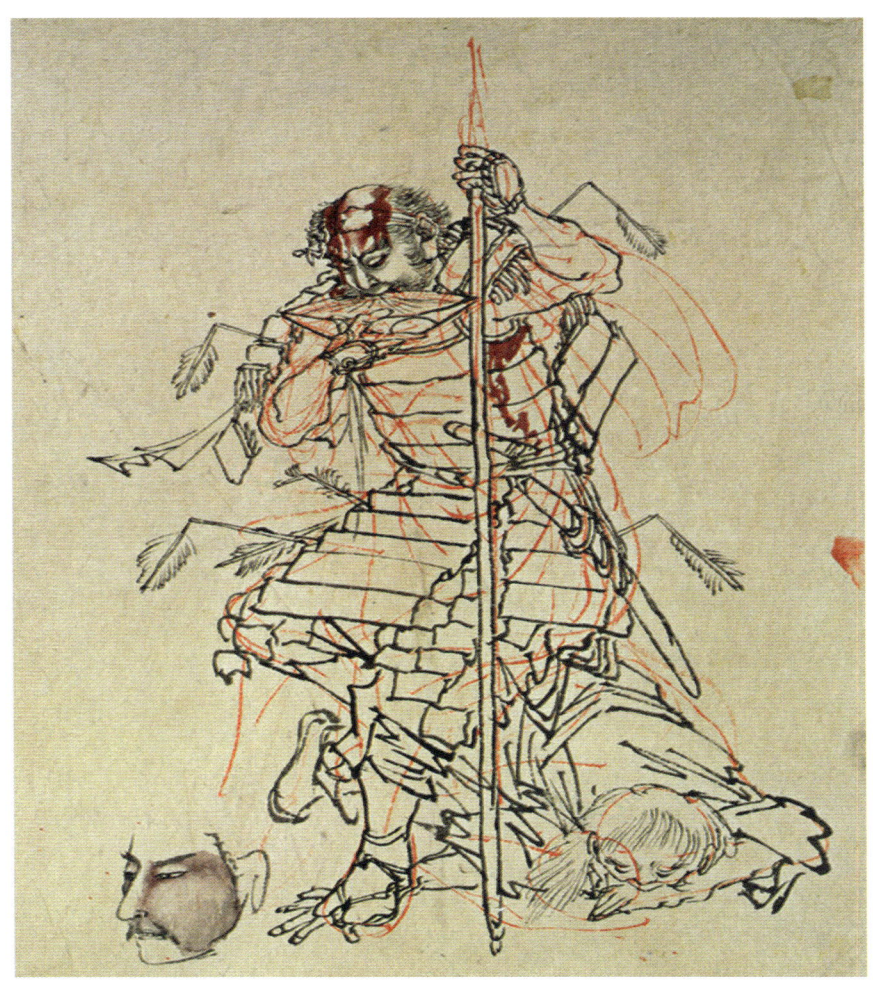

A samurai drinking sake (*Sake o nomu samurai*).

When you go to see someone who is having a tough time, you should carefully consider what you say to them, as this can reveal a lot about a person. Remember that it is unseemly for a warrior to be unkempt and exhausted. You are of no use to anyone unless you are in high spirits, brimming with the determination to succeed and advance. This attitude will also encourage and inspire others.

(Anecdote 73)

'Legendary Strongman Sakata Kinpira (Kintoki) Drinking Sake',
by Ishikawa Toyonobu (1750).

There is a saying that 'If you wish to see into a person's heart, become ill.' It is cowardly to be friendly toward a person on a daily basis yet drift away when they are sick or in need. When people are going through misfortune, we should nurture our connection with them by paying them a visit and sending letters or gifts. We should never estrange ourselves from someone who has done us a favour in the past. It is in these times that a person's true nature can be known. It seems to me that many people depend on others when they are in need, only to forget about them thereafter.

(*Anecdote 94*)

There are occasions when you will need to ask people for favours or borrow things from them; but do this too many times and it will start to come across as begging. It is best not to ask others for help if you can manage without.

(Anecdote 78)

Yamamoto Jin'uemon said: 'A good warrior is a dependable person, and dependable people are good warriors. I know this through my own experience. Though you won't see them when things are going well for you, you know that they will be there for you when times are tough. Those dependable people are the ones who make good warriors.'

(Anecdote 133)

When engaging in a discussion with someone, make sure to tailor your approach to the person. If you say something that doesn't align with them just because you personally think it's a good thing to say, you will lose their interest.

(Anecdote 150)

We can only be at peace when all people are united as one and allow themselves to be guided by the Way of Harmony. Even if they act in accordance with the greater good, if people are not united in harmony, it will never amount to true loyalty. Being on bad terms with your peers, failing to show your face at small get-togethers and constantly complaining are signs of petty small-mindedness. Even if someone is the last person you want to see, always be welcoming and courteous when you meet, be attentive to their needs and never act as though it is a chore. This world is transient – no one knows what will happen from one minute to the next. It is not good to leave people with a bad impression of you when every moment could be your last. On the other hand, it will not benefit you to come across as shallow or a suck-up.

Be respectful to others, avoid conflict, maintain courtesy and do what is good for others even if it is not good for yourself. Then every time you see someone it will be like the first time all over again, and you will always get along well. The same is true for marriage. If you always treat it like the honeymoon phase, there will be no reason to quarrel.

(Anecdote 164)

Scene during the attack on Kira Yoshinaka's home by the 47 Ronin, with the samurai chasing Kira's guards into the house.

Hosokawa Sumimoto (1489–1520) was a samurai commander who lived during the Muromachi Period (16th century). Traditionally, samurai fought on horseback, usually as mounted archers, a skill at which they were highly adept.

I received a letter from someone on a trip to Edo detailing their entire trip from day one. Many people forget to keep in contact when they are busy and frazzled, so this person is a cut above them all when it comes to this thoughtfulness.

(Anecdote 188)

Samurai charge at the battle of Sekigahara (1600).

Often, you will be knocked down, dragged back and made to look bad by friends who only have your best interests at heart.

(*Anecdote 194*)

'Samurai', Yokohama, 1865, by Felice Beato. Just a few years after Beato made this photograph, the feudal period in Japan ended with the Meiji Restoration. After more than eight centuries of military leadership, the samurai class was officially abolished.

Family Relations, Youth & Aging

家族・若者・老化

Filial piety is to act in accordance with loyalty. They are the same thing. To devote yourself to the good of others is to make sure that others are fulfilling their roles.

(Anecdote 19)

Once a young boy attempted to read a book before a priest. The priest called to the other children: 'Everyone, gather around and listen. It is hard to read aloud when lacking an audience.' The priest was impressed by the youth and said that all the children should endeavour to have such an attitude in all they did.

(Anecdote 30)

Nowadays, the youth talk like idiots, they deal with things with words alone and avoid anything that could be the slightest bit difficult. Young people should think twice about this.

(Anecdote 36)

Some people serve as retainers until they are in their 60s or 70s, whereas I left service at the age of 42. Really, my time in this world has been very short and, for that, I am thankful. Thinking about it now, if I had continued serving all through my life, it would have been a real hardship. Yet, somehow, I have lived in comfort these

'Bathtime' (*Gyōzui*), by Kitagawa Utamaro (ca. 1801).

past 14 years, and people have treated me very well. When I reflect on this, I wonder how I can face the world with a clear conscience; I feel guilty, like people's kindness has been wasted on me.

(*Anecdote 37*)

There is a man who has gone senile in his old age. People invite him places and he goes and speaks, imparting his wisdom. For the past several years, his only wish has been to help others, and he has fervently applied himself to the public good. Because of his devotion, he has been of great use to the lord. People tend toward their strengths as their mind is lost to age, which means that those who become obsessed with helping others are in a dangerous position. It is more respectable to stay close to home in one's old age and this will be a more fitting end to one's life.

(Anecdote 41)

There is a proper way to raise a samurai child. Firstly, courage should be instilled from infancy, and threats, wheedling or deception should never be used even in passing. Cowardice instilled at an early age will become a lifelong disadvantage. Parents who say frightening things to their children, make them scared of thunder and going out in the dark, and who try to stop them from crying, do not realize what they are doing. Severely scolding a young child can cause them to become withdrawn. You must also make sure that they do not develop any bad habits. Once a habit is formed, it is extremely hard to break, no matter how much you chide them. Gradually introduce them to proper speech and etiquette and make sure they aren't greedy. Teach them well, and the average child will naturally mature in all aspects.

'Mother and Son by a Mosquito Net', by Suzuki Harunobu (ca. 1769).

It naturally follows that the child of unhappy parents is an unhappy one. Every living creature is affected by the things they see and hear from the moment they are born. Also, if the mother is not careful, she can affect the relationship between the father and child. If the mother spoils the child, when the father admonishes them the mother will take the child's side, and it will sour the child's relationship with the father.

(*Anecdote 85*)

Bad relationships between retired and current lords, fathers and sons, and brothers generally result from greed.

(Anecdote 126)

Simply rising through the ranks at a young age and being appointed to a position of authority will not fulfil you. Even if you are naturally smart, you will lack experience and people will not accept you.

It is better, instead, to take your time, securing your success from around the age of 50. Those whose success appears to have been earned slowly are also seen as accomplished people.

Additionally, even if your fortunes are failing, an ambitious person will quickly recover, knowing that it is through no fault of their own.

(Anecdote 127)

Be aggressive and proactive until the age of 40; once you reach 50, it is more appropriate to slow down and take a more mellow approach.

(Anecdote 149)

Sanjuroku ju sen, by Mizuno Toshikata (1866–1908). As they emerge from the public bath in the background, we share an informal moment with a samurai family. Their attire is simple, and their hair, still wet, is plainly combed and unadorned. The servant, carrying a drying cloth and a long pipe, is easily identifiable through his plain and short garment, his bare feet, and his position behind the family.

'Ichikawa Danjūrō VII Preparing New Year's Gifts', by Utagawa Kunisada (ca. 1830).

In this world, there are many people who teach moral lessons, but few who like to listen to them. There are even fewer who follow these teachings. But once you reach the age of 30, no one will even try to teach you. When the path to learning is closed off, we become selfish, doomed to repeat our mistakes again and again, growing ever more foolish and wasting our lives. Do whatever you can to become close to those who know the Way and take their lessons on board.

(*Anecdote 154*)

It is said that great talents mature late. Real success takes at least 20 to 30 years to achieve. If you try to rush things, you will end up speaking on matters outside your expertise. People will see you as a promising young upstart and it will go to your head; you will become smug and self-congratulatory while acting rashly. This leads to you coming across as superficial and a suck-up, and you will be criticized behind your back. Unless you are willing to put in the hard work of training and allow other people to support you, you will not be of any use.

(*Anecdote 156*)

The elderly tend to reveal their inherent characteristics. People can hide things about themselves when they are still full of vitality, but as they grow weaker, their true colours are revealed, leading to humiliation. Though it may manifest in different ways, this decline happens to everyone who passes the age of 60. Thinking that you won't lose your wits only shows that you already have. Ittei was a particularly stubborn old man. Convinced that he could hold up the family all on his own, he went around ingratiating himself with the illustrious families, looking like a senile old man. I think it happens to the best of us. Looking back on it now, he was a prime example of a washed-up old man. Having had a close-up view of such senility, when I started feeling the burden of old age, I decided to stop going out in public. We have to be able to foresee what lies in store for us.

(*Anecdote 168*)

'Chinese Warrior Carrying a Child upon His Shoulders', by Totoya Hokkei (ca. 1825).

'Ichikawa Danjūrō V and His Family' – print by Torii Kiyonaga (1752–1815).

I heard from a priest at Ryūtaiji temple that a diviner in Kamigata once said that even a Buddhist monk can't hope for success in life before turning 40. There are always mistakes to be made. Confucius is not the only person to have found truth in the idea that things become clear at 40. Whether you're wise or foolish, by the time you reach 40 you will have gained experience commensurate with your stature, and there will be no more confusion.

(Anecdote 171)

It is said that when seeking a loyal subject, you should call at the house of a dutiful child. We should all strive to perform our filial duty with all our heart. We can have many regrets after our parents are gone. Though there are plenty of retainers who will do their very best to perform their duties for their lord, there are few who fulfil their duty to their parents.

True loyalty is something that can only be understood if a person has unreasonable parents or an unreasonable lord. If you are a good person, even strangers will be friendly toward you. There is a saying that pine trees flourish after the frost.

(Anecdote 176)

Until you reach 40, it is better to value being aggressively proactive over relying on wisdom or good sense. Depending on the person and their status, someone who lacks this strength may not make an impression even after the age of 40.

(*Anecdote 186*)

Above & opposite: 'A Group of Brave Warriors of the Takeda Clan', by Sadahide (1807–73). Part of a triptych, this illustration shows how a 16th-century warrior suited-up before going into battle. Beside each warrior is a number (in a yellow circle), his name (in a red cartouche), and the name of the item he is putting on.

The resolve of people in the past ran deep. When war raged, any man aged between 13 and 60 was called to serve. And so, the old men hid their ages.

(*Anecdote 191*)

As *daimyo* of the Ogi domain, Nabeshima Mototake rose to a high position within the Tokugawa shogunate under shogun Tokugawa Tsunayoshi.

Material Possessions & Physical Presentation

財産・姿形

Japanese funeral customs: a kneeling, red-robed Buddhist priest chants before the picture of a family ancestor (watercolour, ca. 1880).

When a lord passes away, people rush to take his belongings for their own. From this, we can discern that human nature is not to be trusted. There is nothing more discourteous than to take a lord's once-treasured possessions, toss them into boxes and bags, and put a price tag on them or pilfer them for use in one's own household. Even if they somehow avoid a curse from the deceased, I can't imagine they will live in peace. There is no honour in mere surface-level servitude.

(*Anecdote 10*)

These days, the moment people hear that there is an estate sale, they immediately covet those items for themselves; they force themselves into the homes of the townspeople to partake of their hospitality; they go shopping as a diversion. Such behaviour is unbecoming of a samurai.

(Anecdote 11)

Yamazaki Kurando was a man who never, in his entire life, took any item that was left over from an estate or put up for auction, nor did he impose himself upon the homes of the common people. This is how a retainer should properly conduct themselves.

(Anecdote 19)

There is one thing that can disadvantage you as a retainer, and that is to be wealthy. A person who has little will be free from this flaw. Another is to be a clever person who nitpicks on subpar work. This never goes well. Unless you take on the world with full acknowledgement that it is full of mistakes, you will look upon it with bitterness, and people will not think kindly of you. No matter how good a person you are, you can't demonstrate this if others do not accept you. This, too, will put you at a disadvantage.

(Anecdote 56)

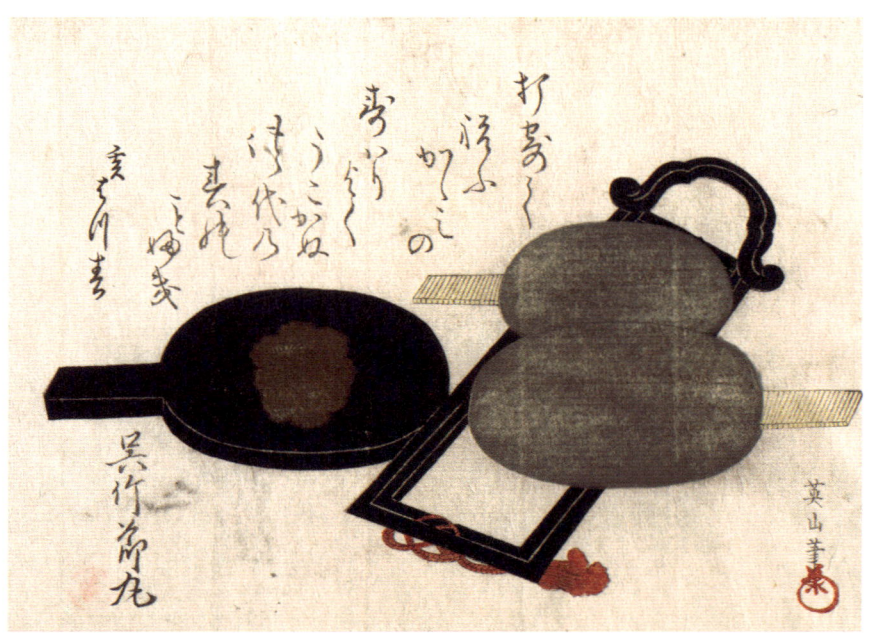

'Mirror and Stand', by Kikugawa Eizan (ca. 1815).

There are many people whose homes or belongings might not seem to match their status. But there's nothing wrong with splurging a little on some things such as fans, tissues, stationery, bedding and so on.

(*Anecdote 57*)

The world has changed in the past 30 years, and young samurai these days talk only about women, money, profit, loss, gossip, fashion and sex. It seems that their friendships depend on these topics. We are truly falling into ruin. In the past, even the youth didn't talk of such things because they didn't have a vulgar bone in their body. If an older person happened to say something untoward, they would recognize and regret their mistake.

I think that this degeneration is happening because the world has become so gaudy these days that people only care about money. But you can get by just fine if you refrain from indulging in extravagances beyond your means.

It is also shallow to praise today's young people for being frugal or having a good home. It is dishonourable to be overly concerned with not wasting money, and a person without honour is a coward.

(Anecdote 63)

The secret to improving your appearance and posture is to look in the mirror regularly and make corrections. People tend to avoid looking in the mirror, and so their physical presentation is lacking.

To improve your speech, step away from work and practise at home. Improving your writing requires revising your sentences, even in a single-line memo. In both the spoken and written word, you should be steady and unhurried. It is said that in Kamigata people are taught that when writing a letter, they should imagine that it will end up on the recipient's wall.

(Anecdote 89)

Make sure to look in the mirror often when working on improving and maintaining your physical appearance.

(*Anecdote 108*)

Beware of boasting and extravagance when things are going well for you. It's in these times that we need to be more restrained in our everyday life, or else we will find ourselves falling behind. The people who get carried away when times are good are the same people who will be worn down when times are tough.

(*Anecdote 175*)

My father Jin'uemon used to say: 'A retainer should use a toothpick even when he has not eaten. Wear a dog's skin on the inside and a tiger's without.' A samurai should take care of their outside appearance while being frugal on the inside. Most people seem to have it the wrong way around.

(*Anecdote 146*)

When things are going well for you, take extra care to watch out for boasting and extravagance. In fact, be twice as cautious as usual to avoid this danger.

(*Anecdote 201*)

Heike and Genji forces clash on the rocky shore at Ishibashiyama within sight of a moonlit Mt. Fuji.

It is good etiquette to keep your armour in good condition. However, as with anything, you should only have as much as you need. Fukahori Inosuke was a good example of this. If you are a person of high rank with a large retinue, you will need a stockpile of money set aside in preparation for war. Okabe Kunai had a bag made for each person in his retinue, wrote their names on them and filled them with the appropriate amount of military funds. This was a very meaningful gesture.

(*Anecdote 202*)

This 1780 illustration shows the actors Nakamura Nakazo I as Chinzei Hachiro Tametomo disguised as a pilgrim (left), and Ichikawa Danjuro V as Kazusa no Gorobei Tadamitsu (right), in the play 'Returning Home in Splendor' (*Kitekaeru Nishiki no Wakayaka*).

General Advice

雑談

We are all puppets.

(*Anecdote 42*)

A man returned to his hometown after several years in the city of Osaka and reported in at the local governmental office. When he spoke in the Osakan dialect, the people there mocked and laughed at him.

I think that when spending a long time in the big cities of Edo or Osaka, you should make sure to use your own local dialect on a regular basis. It is only natural for our own feelings to shift and be coloured by our surroundings, and for us to start looking down on our birthplace as provincial; but it is insipid and stupid to see how something is done elsewhere and envy it as a better way. The fact that your hometown is rustic and simplistic is, in fact, what makes it special.

Trying to imitate the customs of elsewhere will only render you a fake.

(*Anecdote 49*)

This print depicts samurai Shibata Katsuie with a drawn sword in his right hand and a fan in his left hand (by Sakamaki Kogyo, 1899).

Here are a few of Yamamoto Jin'uemon's teachings:

If you can see a thing from one direction, you can see it from eight.

When giving a speech or telling a story, always look your audience in the eye.

A bow at the start will suffice; speaking with your head lowered is careless.

A true warrior is someone who can be relied upon.

(*Anecdote 60*)

Daoist Immortal with dragon (late 19th century).

Some things should not be undertaken hastily. One example is when moving house. There is such a thing as good timing, and it is important to practise self-restraint until it arrives. Then, when the right time comes, move quickly and without hesitation. There are times when thinking too long and dithering on something leads to failure. Similarly, there are times when it is best to throw yourself in fully from the start. There are also times when it is instead better to test people's patience and do things in the most boring way. In those instances, how you use your words will be key. Either way, the important thing is to commit to an approach and maintain your focus.

(Anecdote 67)

At a recent important meeting, someone stepped forward to challenge the person in charge and laid out a detailed account of their thoughts. But when their proposal was agreed to by the group, they said that the agreement had come too quickly and that this made the people seem fickle and unreliable.

(Anecdote 76)

In this 1763 print by Torii Kiyomitsu children play-act a *daimyo* procession.

In the Tang Dynasty, there was a man who loved dragons. All his clothing, utensils and so on were adorned with images of dragons. Moved by the depths of the man's love, one day the Dragon God sent a real dragon to appear at his window. The man was so startled that he fainted. There are many people who will talk big to anyone who will listen, yet when they're made to put their money where their mouth is, they act completely contrary.

(*Anecdote 81*)

Ishida Ittei said: 'If you wish for something hard enough, it will come true. There used to be no matsutake mushrooms in our domain. People who tasted them in Kamigata wished for us to have them in our domain, and now our lands are filled with them. In the future, I hope that we will be able to grow cypress trees in our mountains. I think that is what the future holds, as everyone is wishing for it. Everyone should have something they wish to manifest.'

(*Anecdote 103*)

It is foolish to call something that is out of the ordinary a 'mystery' and treat it as an omen of things to come. The appearance of the sun and the moon side by side, comets, odd cloud formations, strange lights, snow in June; though these events are rare, they do occur once every 50 or 100 years or so due to the cosmic forces of yin and yang. If it was unusual for the sun to rise in the east and set in the west, it would be deemed a mystery if it happened. People will look at the clouds and see an omen, become convinced that something bad is going to happen and then be vindicated when some natural disaster happens, as it surely will somewhere in the world. Because they are always waiting for something bad to happen, bad things will happen.

(*Anecdote 105*)

Those who have a sharp mind for accounting tend to become cowardly and corrupt. This is because accounting is concerned with profit and loss, and so they see everything from a perspective of loss and gain. Death is seen as a loss and life as a gain; therefore death is undesirable, and this fear of death leads to cowardice. Furthermore, a learned person can hide their cowardice and greed behind wit and eloquence, which leads others to overestimate them.

(Anecdote 112)

In writing calligraphy, the most important thing is to follow the correct form. However, this alone will result in your work looking stiff and unrefined. There is something that transcends mere preciseness of form; not just in calligraphy, but in all things.

(Anecdote 91)

It's okay to get involved with unexpected, unconnected things so long as you don't lose the main thread. In the end, there are important things to be discovered in these digressions, in the branches and leaves as it were. Sometimes the overall worth of a situation can be found in the small details.

(Anecdote 170)

'Noh Mask of an Old Man' (Asakurajō), ca. 18th century.

Shikibu taught: 'When reading aloud, read from your stomach; if you read from your mouth, your voice will fail you.'

(*Anecdote 174*)

Ittei said that writing is the art of making the paper, brush and ink work together when all they want is to be separate.

(*Anecdote 177*)

'Nobleman Making Calligraphy', by Yashima Gakutei (ca. 1830).

Ittei said: 'If you asked me to sum up what it means to "do good", I would say that it is to endure suffering. Without enduring suffering, nothing is good.'

(Anecdote 184)

When we look back on the past, there are many theories and many things that cannot be determined – it is okay if these things remain unknown. Lord Sanenori said: 'Some of the things we don't understand will eventually become clear. Some we can figure out for ourselves; others we will never understand. That's what makes things interesting.' This is a profound observation. The past is full of deep mysteries that will never come to light. At the same time, that which can be easily understood tends to be shallow.

(Anecdote 203)

Sources & Further Reading

Bennett, Alexander, trans. *Hagakure: The Secret Wisdom of the Samurai.* Tuttle Publishing, 2014.

Day, Stacey B. *The Wisdom of Hagakure.* Kyushu University Press, 1994.

Kanno, Kakumyō, Takeshi Kurihara and Kei Kizawa. *Shinkōtei Zenyakuchū Hagakure Jou* (Hagakure Revised Annotated Translation Vol. 1). Kodansha, 2017.

Mishima, Yukio. *Mishima on Hagakure: The Samurai Ethic and Modern Japan.* Penguin, 1979.

Steben, Barry D, trans. *The Art of the Samurai: Yamamoto Tsunetomo's Hagakure.* Duncan Baird Publishers, 2008.

Wilson, William Scott, trans. *Hagakure: The Book of the Samurai.* Shambhala Publications, 2012.

PICTURE CREDITS

Alamy: 12 (The Protected Art Archive), 15 (Science History Images), 24 (CPA Media), 56/57 (Penta Springs), 81 (Pump Park Vintage Photography), 84/85 (Pump Park Vintage Photography), 86 (CPA Media), 112 (Interfoto), 122 (CPA Media)

Getty Images: 22 (Pictures From History), 90/91 (Werner Forman), 102/103 (Burstein Collection), 105, 107 & 148 (Heritage Images)

Library of Congress: 16, 28, 43, 55, 63, 68, 88, 98/99, 108, 117

Metropolitan Museum of Art, New York: 18, 21, 30, 33, 37, 39, 51, 52/53, 58, 60, 64, 67, 70, 73, 78/79, 82, 115, 118, 121, 124, 127, 129, 132, 135, 136, 144, 152, 154, 157, 158

Public Domain: 6, 8, 10, 110, 123, 140

Walters Art Museum, Baltimore: 34, 77, 94, 97, 131, 138/139, 147, 151

Wellcome Collection: 26/27, 40, 44/45, 48, 100/101, 142

Background images by Aryu/dreamstime